Inside the Mind of Emma Watson

FRANK JOHNSON

Copyright © 2014 Frank Johnson

All rights reserved.

ISBN: 1502845229
ISBN-13: 978-1502845221

CONTENTS

1	Introduction	1
2	About Acting	3
3	About Herself	9
4	About Life	21
5	About Other People	23
6	Appearance & Fashion	27
7	General Opinions & Philosophy	33
8	On Fame	35
9	On Love & Romance	39

INTRODUCTION

Best known, of course, for her role as Hermione in the Harry Potter films, Emma Watson has known fame since just nine years old. Yet, in contrast to many childhood stars, she has managed to remain grounded and has never let her fame go to her head.

Having won several major awards, Emma has since moved on from the Harry Potter franchise to star in other major films, and has also become somewhat of a sex symbol (though she would probably disapprove of this title!).

Outside of the acting world, Emma is known for her love of life and travelling. She is probably one of the best examples of somebody who has managed not to let her fame get in the way of leading a 'normal' life, pursuing an education and qualifying with a degree in English literature.

There is much to be admired about this genuine character, and she has been a much quoted figure within the media.

This book brings together some of her most interesting quotes on a variety of subjects.

ABOUT ACTING

"Hermione uses all these big long tongue twister words. I don't know what she's going on about half the time!"

*

"Acting never was about the money for me... Maybe in 10 years, I'll be able to appreciate the fact that I am financially stable and independent and I don't have to make bad choices. I can be very picky."

*

"I mean, I have done scenes with animals, with owls, with bats, with cats, with special effects, with thespians, in the freezing cold, in the pouring rain, boiling hot; I've done press with every syndication, every country; I've done interviews with people dressed up as cows - there's honestly nothing that's gonna intimidate me!"

*

"I stole a piece of the chess set on the first film. I took a piece of the treasure out of Bellatrix's vault on this film. And I've taken my wand and I've got my cloak."

*

"I could be 100 years old and in my rocker, but I'll still be very proud that I was part of the 'Harry Potter' films."

*

"I think when I was younger I wasn't really sure if I wanted to act, so I played around with a few different ideas. I wasn't sure whether I might want to write or whether I might want to do something in fashion."

*

"I don't know, I'd love to try some theater. That's my other thing. I'd love to do some Shakespeare."

*

"Hermione is so close to who I am as a person that I've never really had to research a role. I'm literally rediscovering what it means to be an actress."

*

"I have felt for the last 10 years I have had this battle; I've been fighting so hard to have an education. It's been this uphill struggle. I was Warner Bros' pain in the butt. I was their scheduling conflict. I was the one who made life difficult."

*

"As an actress I take roles I find interesting."

*

"If anyone else played Hermione, it would actually kill

me."

*

"Now, honestly, every movie set that I go on, I walk onto set with the confidence that there is nothing that they can throw at me that's gonna surprise me."

*

"I think the actresses who are really successful are the ones who are comfortable in their own skins and still look human."

*

"I wasn't one of those girls who always dreamed of being an actress. I went to a normal school and then these film auditioners turned up when I was nine. Then I just fell into this whirlwind."

*

"I just loved performing. It just made me feel alive. It's scary, but that's part of it. I think it's important to have that extra adrenaline. It gives you that extra zing."

*

"Being an actress, I find myself people-watching and I can be quite shy."

*

"I think when you take away all, like, the premieres and press stuff and all the special effects, then you just come down to the fact that it's all about acting, and I think that has been the best bit for me."

ABOUT HERSELF

"I'm not going to school just for the academics - I wanted to share ideas, to be around people who are passionate about learning."

*

"I don't want other people to decide who I am. I want to decide that for myself."

*

"I like books that aren't just lovely but that have memories in themselves. Just like playing a song, picking up a book again that has memories can take you back to another place or another time."

*

"Yes, I will put it out there - I will work for anyone for free if they're prepared to make their clothing Fair Trade and organic. It's really hard to get people interested in it."

*

"When I haven't been working I've tried to travel a lot."

*

"I've always been like that; I give 100 percent. I can't do it any other way."

*

"I still have friends from primary school. And my two best girlfriends are from secondary school. I don't have to explain anything to them. I don't have to apologize for anything. They know. There's no judgment in any way."

*

"I'm very crafty! One time I made a television set out of a cardboard box - Everybody thought it was a lark! This was the beginning of a love affair with the arts."

*

"I was very keen. I was super-eager to please and be good. And I was always kind of bossy."

*

"If I hadn't done 'Harry Potter,' I would have gone and done years of art. I really do love it, and I'd love to write."

*

"I just try and surround myself, for the biggest proportion of time that I can, with people who make me feel normal, because constantly feeling abnormal is quite difficult."

*

"I feel like a voodoo doll. It's grim. It's gross."

*

"The difficulty for me is that I'm interested in so many different things. I could never really imagine myself doing one thing, and I'm pretty sure that I'll end up doing four or five different things."

*

"It's almost like the better I do, the more my feeling of inadequacy actually increases, because I'm just going, 'Any moment, someone's going to find out I'm a total fraud, and that I don't deserve any of what I've achieved. I can't possibly live up to what everyone thinks I am and what everyone's expectations of me are.'"

*

"And I always keep cards people send me. I have a whole wall covered with them."

*

"Let's be honest, I have enough money to never have to work again."

*

"I'm going to do what I want to do. I'm going to be who I really am. I'm going to figure out what that is."

*

"I'm a perfectionist, so my bossiness definitely comes out."

*

"I've probably earned the right to screw up a few times. I don't want the fear of failure to stop me from doing what I really care about."

*

"All I can do is follow my instincts, because I'll never please everyone."

*

"But sometimes I've felt a little constrained by that idea of who I'm meant to be."

*

"I really want to write a novel. I also want to learn to play the mandolin."

*

"I'm really interested in modern history, but to fulfill a History degree at Brown you have to do modern and pre-modern."

*

"I guess what really forms you as a person is what you do within your family to receive love or attention. In my family, what you had to do to receive attention was to have good conversation at the dinner table or for me to do well at school, and those were really my focuses because that was what was valued the most."

*

"I didn't come from a background of films. I didn't even really ever watch films. The fact is, my parents weren't into that stuff, and neither was I."

*

"I have to really enjoy the good things because it makes the bad things OK."

*

"I want to be a Renaissance woman. I want to paint, and I want to write, and I want to act, and I want to just do everything."

*

"I genuinely haven't really had a rebellious phase. I think it's just because of the way I was brought up. I think it's because I left home when I was ten years old."

*

"Field hockey is my strongest sport, and if I lose a game, I take a long, hot bath and moan about it."

*

"I dance a lot and I run and do yoga and play field hockey and tennis. I like to be active. I don't always have time for that stuff, but I do always feel better afterward."

*

"I love painting and have a need to do it."

*

"My grandma said - when I was really young and I'd sing along to the radio - why do you sing in an American accent? I guess it was because a lot of the music I was listening to had American vocalists."

*

"I'm a very heady person; I'm in my head a lot."

*

"I just feel like if I start opening the door to talking about my university experience, then people just kind of... own everything. There was a lot of stuff a couple of years ago saying that I was bullied at Brown and awful things like that, none of which were true."

*

"I have collections of quirky things from places I've been to, like a set of Russian dolls."

*

"I don't think my dad really knew what to do with me, as a daughter. He treated me like a boy; my brother and I were treated the same. He didn't do kid stuff. There were no kid's menus; you weren't allowed to order off the kid's menu at dinner - we had to try something from the adult menu."

*

"I want to avoid becoming too styled, too 'done' and too generic. You see people as they go through their career, and they just become more and more like everyone else. They start out with something individual about them, but it gets lost."

*

"As a child, I loved being onstage. I loved singing, I loved the lights, I loved the adrenaline. I even loved learning lines. I was completely obsessive."

*

"I don't want the fear of failure to stop me from doing what I really care about."

*

"With 'Harry Potter,' I've been all over the world. I probably wouldn't have gone to New York so young if it weren't for the films."

*

"I paint and I draw and I write and I do other things too, and recently some people at school were asking if I'd ever publish any of my work. But I almost feel like

I would have to publish it under another name because there's a definition of me out there that feels kind of stuck in the moment when it was formed."

*

"I threw my 20th birthday party at Brown, and I didn't even have to say to anyone not to put pictures on Facebook. Not a single picture went up. That was when I knew I'd found a solid group of friends, and I felt like I belonged."

*

"It sounds so geeky, but I really do like studying and reading, and if I'm not working on 'Harry Potter,' then my greatest relaxation is to sit with a book."

*

"To be honest, I've always had far too much freedom. I had a job when I was 10. I started living on my own when I was 17 or 18. I've earned my own money; I've traveled the world. What would I rebel against?"

*

"I really love animals and enjoy working with them."

*

"I always have several books on the go at any one moment, so it's no good you asking 'What's on the bedside table at the moment, Emma?' because often I can't even see the table!"

ABOUT LIFE

"The entertainment industry is pretty nuts, and having had that experience outside of it and going to university has really made a big difference. It's important to me to feel like I have my own life."

*

"I have had no control over my life. I have lived in a complete bubble. They found me and picked me for the part. And now I'm desperately trying to find my way through it."

*

"It's a journey and the sad thing is you only learn from experience, so as much as someone can tell you things, you have to go out there and make your own mistakes in order to learn."

ABOUT OTHER PEOPLE

"I am literally obsessed with Lena Dunham. She's, like, my favorite person in the world. I follow her on Twitter; I read her every day."

*

"I love Karl Lagerfeld. I worship him. I was brought up in Paris, and my mum used to wear a lot of Chanel. I love the brand."

*

"I have a real thing for Mexican directors. And I love Guillermo del Toro and Alejandro Gonzalez Inarritu."

*

"I've always been fascinated by Elizabeth Taylor, and I had read that her first kiss happened on a film set, which actually made me a little sad. You need to have normal experiences of your own."

*

"My cinematic crush has been pretty much the same since I was 12: Kevin Costner."

*

"In terms of men I fancy, I think the actor James Franco is gorgeous. But I find it odd to be described as a sex symbol myself."

*

"I would love to persuade Christopher Bailey to get even just a section of Burberry that's, like, organic or free trade. I love him, he's a very good person and an amazing designer, and I have a lot of respect and time for him."

*

"Dan Radcliffe and Rupert Grint to me are like a pair of warm-hearted brothers."

APPEARANCE & FASHION

"As I've got older, and since I cut all my hair off, I've felt a bit more liberated about trying different things out."

*

"I'm a multidimensional person and that's the freedom of fashion: that you're able to reinvent yourself through how you dress and how you cut your hair or whatever."

*

"I'm a real Londoner. We have very grey weather in London, and I think it encourages a very eclectic and crazy fashion sense. I mix high-street stuff with more high-end fashion, and I love vintage."

*

"I don't have makeup on all the time, but when I want, I have fun with my friends choosing clothes and putting nail polish on."

*

"I've got about eight pairs of shoes, and that's it."

*

"I don't have perfect teeth, I'm not stick thin. I want to be the person who feels great in her body and can say that she loves it and doesn't want to change anything."

*

"I used to look back at pictures and cringe but actually I'm quite proud that I've had fun with fashion and don't always look perfect. The only regret I have is when I look at something I wore when I was very young and it obviously looks like it belonged to someone else."

*

"I think there's this idea that lipstick is something quite old or something you'd only wear at night."

*

"I try to avoid wearing black because sometimes it's the easy option. But I'm young, so it's nice to be able to play with color and not just wear black all the time. I can save that for when I'm older."

*

"It's quite stressful knowing that every time you walk out the door, someone is going to be giving you a very good look up and down, judging everything you wear."

*

"I do worry about the expectation to look a certain way."

∗

"I find the whole concept of being 'sexy' embarrassing and confusing. If I do a photo-shoot, people desperately want to change me - dye my hair blonder, pluck my eyebrows, give me a fringe. Then there's the choice of clothes. I know everyone wants a picture of me in a mini-skirt. But that's not me."

∗

"It's very hard to describe your own style. And I'm young, so I'm still experimenting. But I think it's quite British and very much about individuality."

∗

"Make-up is actually something I've always really loved."

∗

*"I love fashion. I think it's so important, because it's

how you show yourself to the world."

*

"I like Valentino a lot - they never use actresses in their campaigns."

*

"If I could wear any label forever it would be Burberry. It covers a huge span of stuff. You can't go wrong with a classic trench and a pair of jeans."

*

"I thought, If people are going to write about what I'm wearing, then I would wear young British designers who need the publicity."

*

"I don't really buy designer stuff. I have a few nice things, but I don't really have the occasion to wear couture too often."

FRANK JOHNSON

*

"My idea of sexy is that less is more. The less you reveal the more people can wonder."

GENERAL OPINIONS & PHILOSOPHY

"I've never understood having crushes on people who you don't know in real life."

*

"It's amazing people get so detached from what they eat and what they wear. No one has any contact with how things are made that are put in their body and put in their mouths and I just find it alarming that no one questions it."

ON FAME

"Some days, for some reason, I can't go anywhere, and I'm like, 'That was a mistake,' and other days no one will even notice me."

*

"People don't really understand, but having people stare, and point, and take pictures, even if it is in a positive framework, is quite isolating; there's no two ways about it. You feel a little bit, you know, freakish."

*

"I went from being totally unknown and never acting

professionally to being in a major movie and being very famous. It all happened so quickly, I didn't have any time to work things out. It's been pretty scary at times."

*

"If I went to somewhere busy, I wouldn't last very long. I can't go to a museum - I'll last 10 or 15 minutes in a museum. The problem is that when one person asks for a photograph, then someone sees a flash goes off, then everyone else sort of... it's sort of like a domino effect."

*

"Ignoring fame was my rebellion, in a funny way. I was insistent on being normal and doing normal things. It probably wasn't advisable to go to college in America and room with a complete stranger. And it probably wasn't wise to share a bathroom with eight other people in a coed dorm. Looking back, that was crazy."

*

"My friends are all really nice about my fame, they're just curious really, they ask lots of questions."

*

"I don't consider myself to be a celebrity. I don't fit that mould."

*

"I was working on 'Harry Potter' while I was growing up, and the attention it brought me made me feel quite isolated."

*

"I want to be normal. I really want anonymity."

ON LOVE & ROMANCE

"I would love to not date someone in the same industry as me. Otherwise it becomes what it means to everyone else."

*

"I'm a feminist, but I think that romance has been taken away a bit for my generation. I think what people connect with in novels is this idea of an overpowering, encompassing love - and it being more important and special than anything and everything else."

*

"I like men with quick wit, good conversation and a great sense of humour. I love banter. I want a man to like me for me - I want him to be authentic."

*

"It sounds like a cliche but I also learnt that you're not going to fall for the right person until you really love yourself and feel good about how you are."

*

"I'm very romantic and of course I want to be in love."

*

"When I started dating I had this kind of Romeo and Juliet, fateful romantic idea about love which was almost that you were a victim and there was a lot of pain involved and that was how it should be."

ALSO BY FRANK JOHNSON

INSIDE THE MIND OF CHUCK PALAHNIUK

THE WIT AND WISDOM OF JOSS WHEDON

THE VERY BEST OF MICHAEL MOORE

Made in the USA
Coppell, TX
07 September 2021